HAL•LEONARD

JAZZ PLAY-ALONG®

ok and CD for B♭, E♭, C and Bass Clef Instruments

volume 148

Arranged and Produced by
Mark Taylor

JOHN COLTRANE
FAVORITES | 10 GREAT TUNES

T0061402

BOOK

CD

Cover photo © Alamy

ISBN 978-1-4584-2216-3

HAL•LEONARD®
CORPORATION

7777 W. BLUEMOUND RD. P.O. BOX 13819 MILWAUKEE, WI 53213

Visit Hal Leonard Online at
www.halleonard.com

JOHN COLTRANE FAVORITES

Volume 148

Arranged and Produced by
Mark Taylor

Featured Players:

Graham Breedlove–Trumpet
John Desalme–Saxes
Tony Nalker–Piano
Regan Brough–Bass
Todd Harrison–Drums

Recorded at Bias Studios, Springfield, Virginia
Bob Dawson, Engineer

HOW TO USE THE CD:

Each song has <u>two</u> tracks:

1) Split Track/Melody

Woodwind, Brass, Keyboard, and **Mallet Players** can use this track as a learning tool for melody style and inflection.

Bass Players can learn and perform with this track – remove the recorded bass track by turning down the volume on the LEFT channel.

Keyboard and **Guitar Players** can learn and perform with this track – remove the recorded piano part by turning down the volume on the RIGHT channel.

2) Full Stereo Track

Soloists or **Groups** can learn and perform with this accompaniment track with the RHYTHM SECTION only.

BIG NICK

BY JOHN COLTRANE

CENTRAL PARK WEST

BY JOHN COLTRANE

C VERSION

CD
5 : SPLIT TRACK/MELODY
6 : FULL STEREO TRACK

CHASIN' THE TRANE

BY JOHN COLTRANE

C VERSION

D.S. AL FINE
TAKE REPEAT

LAST X ONLY

LONNIE'S LAMENT

BY JOHN COLTRANE

C VERSION

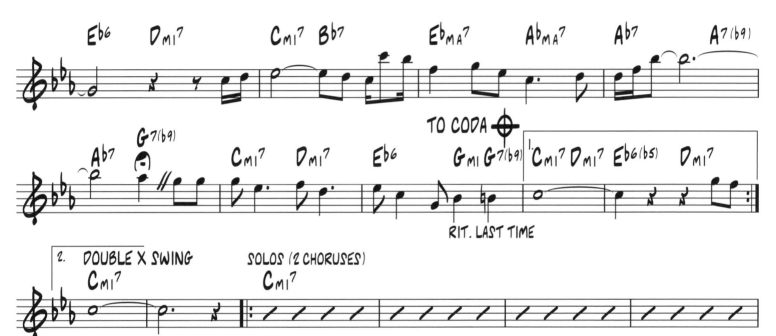

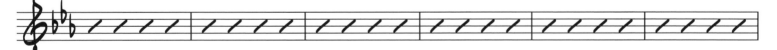

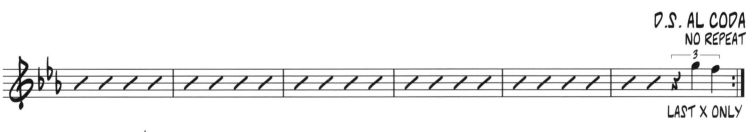

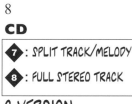

GRAND CENTRAL

BY JOHN COLTRANE

C VERSION

SOLOS (2 CHORUSES)

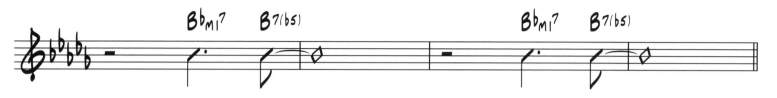

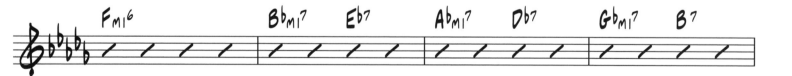

LAST X ONLY - - - - - - - - - - - - - - - - -

CD

9 : SPLIT TRACK/MELODY
10 : FULL STEREO TRACK

C VERSION

LOCOMOTION

BY JOHN COLTRANE

FAST SWING

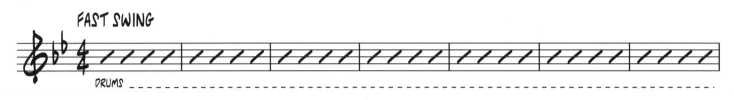

DRUMS

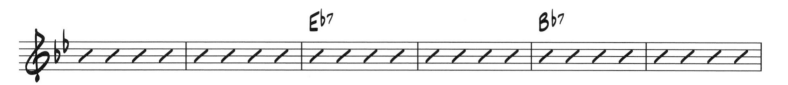

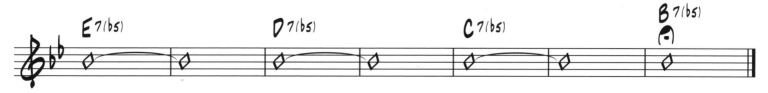

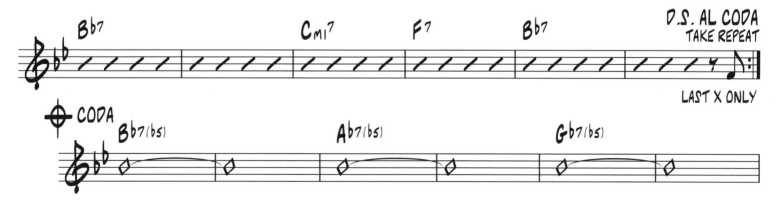

CD

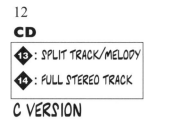

13 : SPLIT TRACK/MELODY
14 : FULL STEREO TRACK

C VERSION

NITA

BY JOHN COLTRANE

FAST SWING

DRUMS

FINE

SOLO BREAK

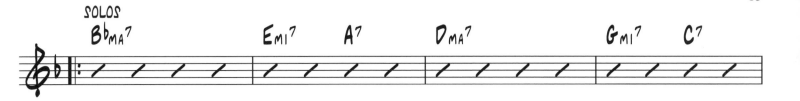

SOLOS

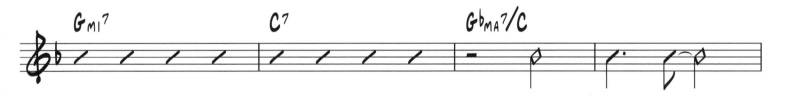

F⁶
D.S. AL FINE
TAKE REPEAT

1. SOLO BREAK   2. N.C.

CD

◆15 : SPLIT TRACK/MELODY
◆16 : FULL STEREO TRACK

SATELLITE

BY JOHN COLTRANE

C VERSION

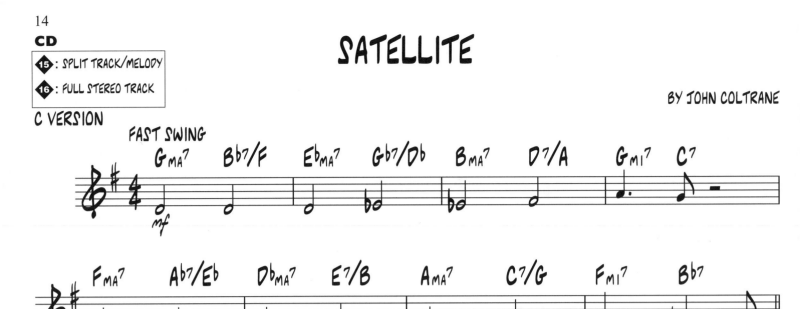

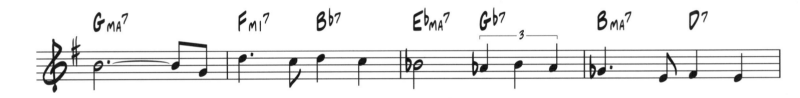

TO CODA ⊕

SOLO (3 CHORUSES)
GMA7 Bb7/F EbMA7 Gb7/Db BMA7 D7/A GMI7 C7 FMA7 Ab7/Eb
DbMA7 E7/B AMA7 C7/G FMI7 Bb7 EbMA7 AMI7 D7
GMI7 AMI7 D7 GMA7 FMI7 Bb7 EbMA7 Gb7
BMA7 D7 GMA7 Bb7/F EbMA7 Gb7/Db BMA7 D7/A GMI7 C7
FMA7 Ab7/Eb DbMA7 E7/B AMA7 C7/G FMI7 Bb7 EbMA7
AMI7 D7 GMA7 AMI7 D7 D7SUS
D.C. AL CODA
CODA
SOLO (PLAY 3X'S)
D7SUS
AbMA7
SLOW
GMA7

CD

19: SPLIT TRACK/MELODY
20: FULL STEREO TRACK

C VERSION

26-2

BY JOHN COLTRANE

MEDIUM SWING

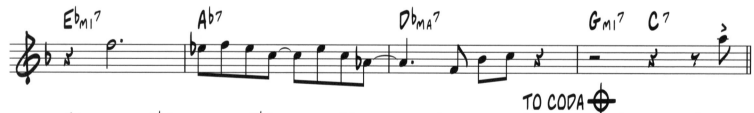

TO CODA ⊕

SOME OTHER BLUES

BY JOHN COLTRANE

BIG NICK

BY JOHN COLTRANE

CENTRAL PARK WEST

BY JOHN COLTRANE

CHASIN' THE TRANE

BY JOHN COLTRANE

Bb VERSION

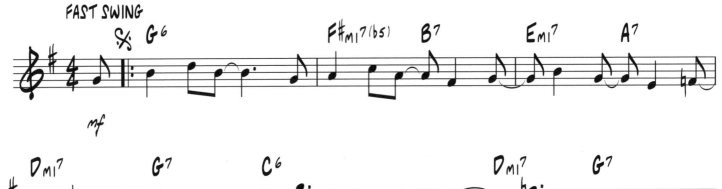

LONNIE'S LAMENT

BY JOHN COLTRANE

CD
11: SPLIT TRACK/MELODY
12: FULL STEREO TRACK

Bb VERSION

MEDIUM BALLAD

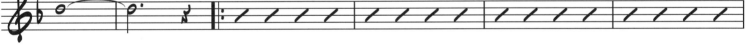

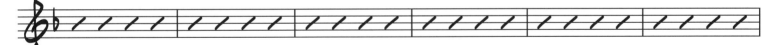

CD

◆7 : SPLIT TRACK/MELODY
◆8 : FULL STEREO TRACK

GRAND CENTRAL

BY JOHN COLTRANE

Bb VERSION

CD

LOCOMOTION

BY JOHN COLTRANE

Bb VERSION

FAST SWING

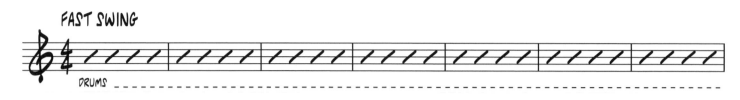

DRUMS

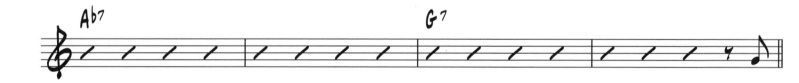

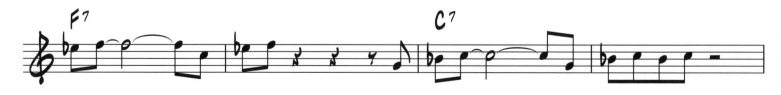

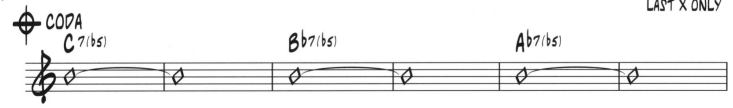

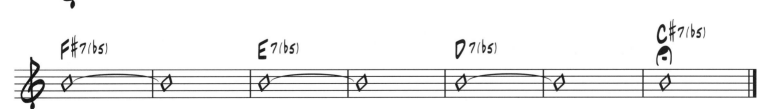

CD

13 : SPLIT TRACK/MELODY
14 : FULL STEREO TRACK

NITA

BY JOHN COLTRANE

Bb VERSION

FAST SWING

DRUMS

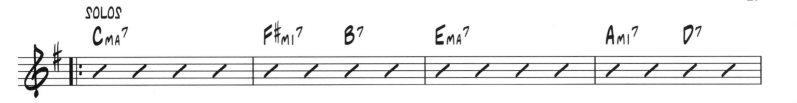

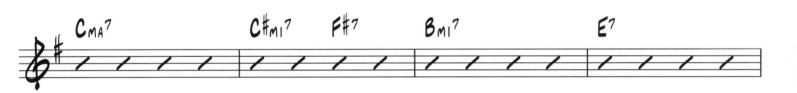

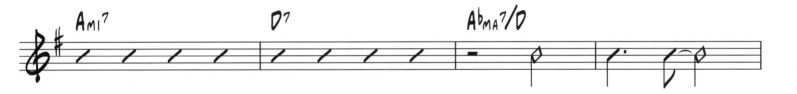

CD

SATELLITE

BY JOHN COLTRANE

Bb VERSION

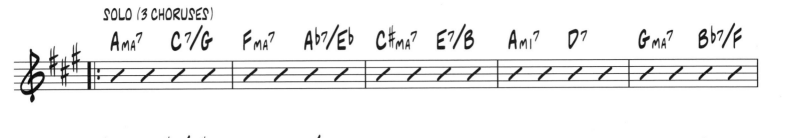

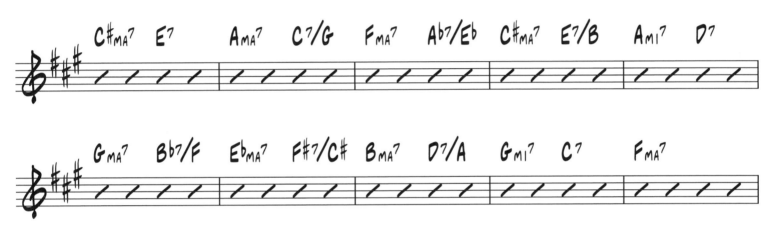

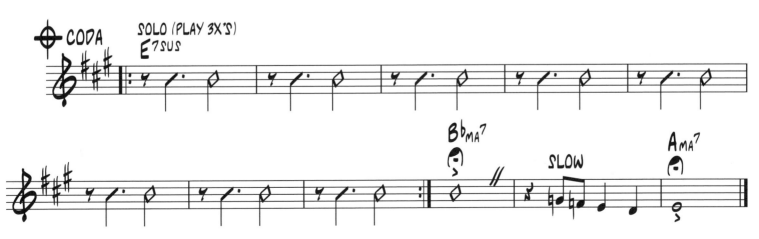

CD

19 : SPLIT TRACK/MELODY
20 : FULL STEREO TRACK

26-2

BY JOHN COLTRANE

Bb VERSION

MEDIUM SWING

CD
- ◆1: SPLIT TRACK/MELODY
- ◆2: FULL STEREO TRACK

BIG NICK

BY JOHN COLTRANE

Eb VERSION

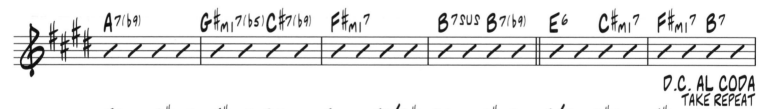

PIANO & BASS _

CENTRAL PARK WEST

BY JOHN COLTRANE

CD
◆ 3: SPLIT TRACK/MELODY
◆ 4: FULL STEREO TRACK

Eb VERSION

CD

CHASIN' THE TRANE

BY JOHN COLTRANE

Eb VERSION

FAST SWING

SOLOS (8 CHORUSES)

LAST X ONLY

LONNIE'S LAMENT

BY JOHN COLTRANE

Eb VERSION

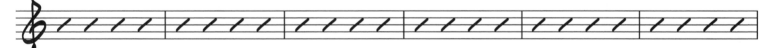

GRAND CENTRAL

BY JOHN COLTRANE

CD
- ◆ 7 : SPLIT TRACK/MELODY
- ◆ 8 : FULL STEREO TRACK

Eb VERSION

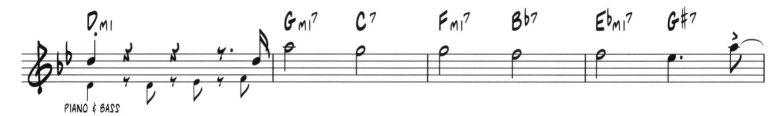

39

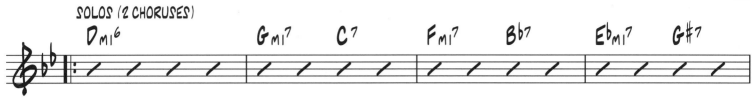

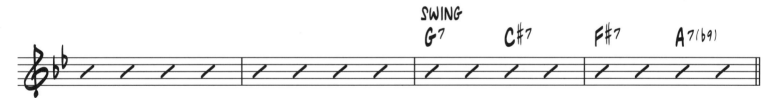

LOCOMOTION

BY JOHN COLTRANE

Eb VERSION

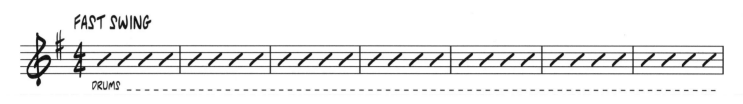

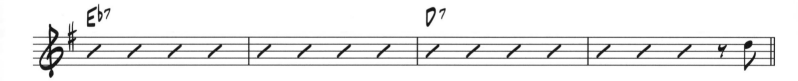

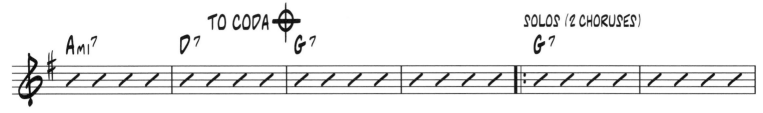

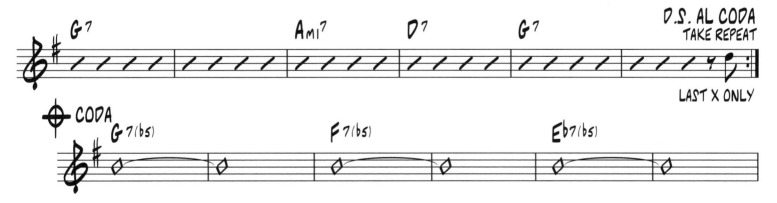

NITA

BY JOHN COLTRANE

Eb VERSION

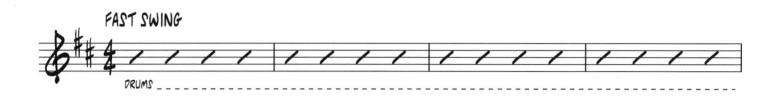

SOLOS
G^MA7   C#MI7   F#7   B^MA7   E^MI7   A7

D^MA7   G#MI7(b5) C#7(b9)   F#MA7   A7   D^MA7   D7

G^MA7   C#MI7   F#7   B^MA7   E^MI7   A7

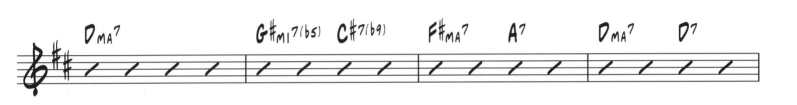

D^MA7   G#MI7(b5) C#7(b9)   F#MA7   A7   D^MA7   D7

G^MA7   G#MI7   C#7   F#MI7   B7

E^MI7   A7   Eb^MA7/A

D6

1. SOLO BREAK   2. N.C.   D.S. AL FINE TAKE REPEAT

CD

15 : SPLIT TRACK/MELODY
16 : FULL STEREO TRACK

SATELLITE

BY JOHN COLTRANE

Eb VERSION

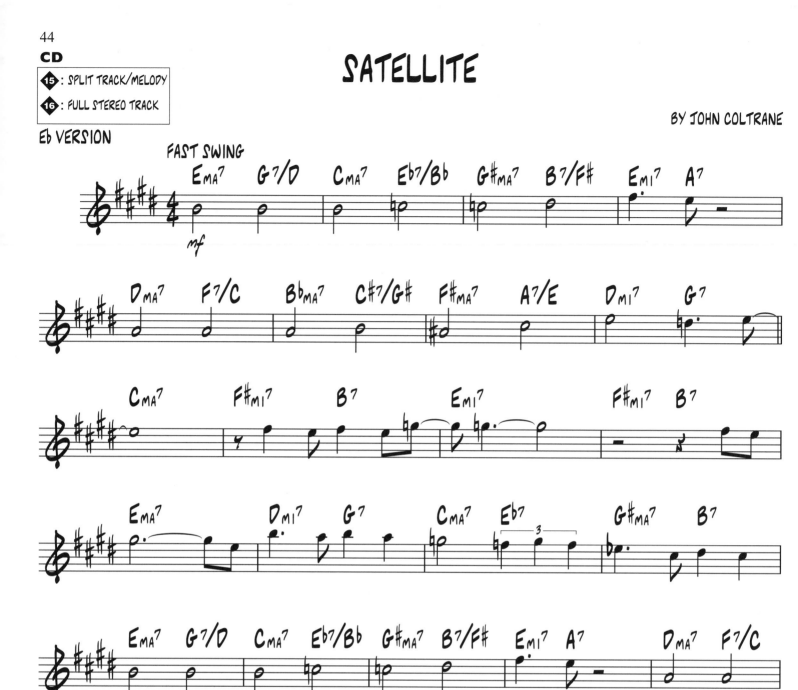

CD

26-2

BY JOHN COLTRANE

Eb VERSION

MEDIUM SWING

TO CODA ✛

SOME OTHER BLUES

CD
17 : SPLIT TRACK/MELODY
18 : FULL STEREO TRACK

BY JOHN COLTRANE

Eb VERSION

SOME OTHER BLUES

BY JOHN COLTRANE

BIG NICK

BY JOHN COLTRANE

CENTRAL PARK WEST

BY JOHN COLTRANE

CD
5: SPLIT TRACK/MELODY
6: FULL STEREO TRACK

CHASIN' THE TRANE

BY JOHN COLTRANE

𝄢: C VERSION

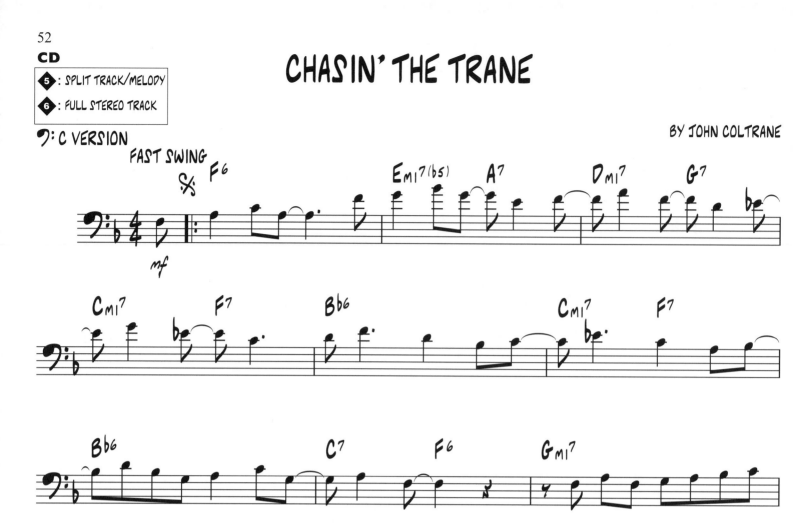

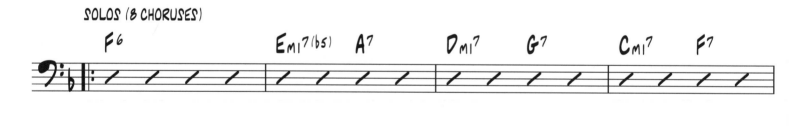

LONNIE'S LAMENT

BY JOHN COLTRANE

CD
- 11 : SPLIT TRACK/MELODY
- 12 : FULL STEREO TRACK

C VERSION

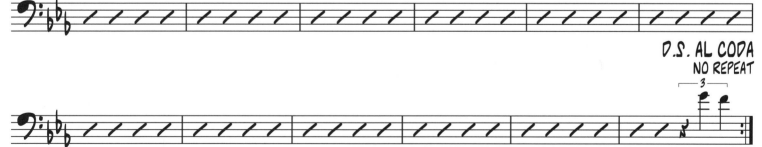

GRAND CENTRAL

BY JOHN COLTRANE

𝄢: C VERSION

FAST SWING

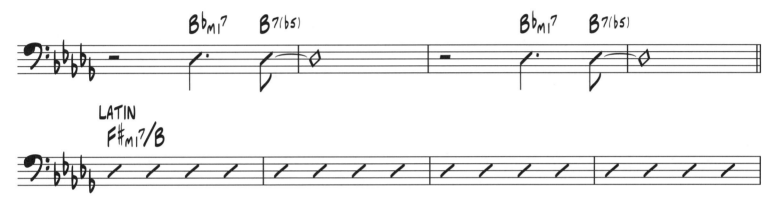

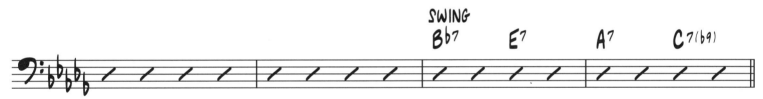

LOCOMOTION

BY JOHN COLTRANE

🎵: C VERSION

FAST SWING

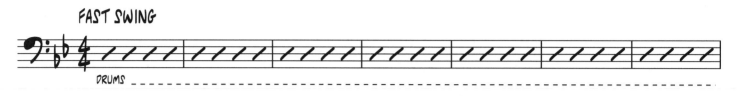

DRUMS

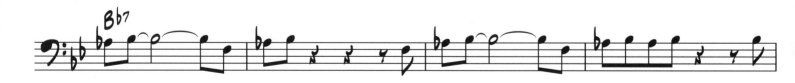

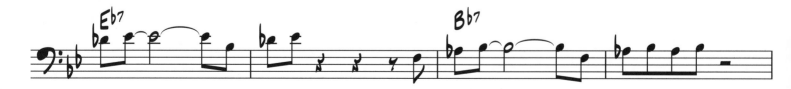

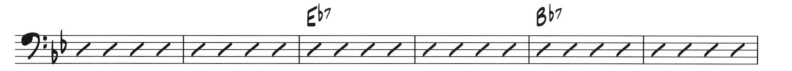

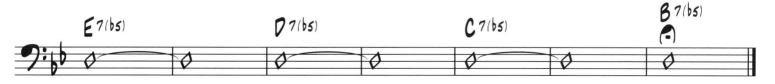

CD

13: SPLIT TRACK/MELODY

14: FULL STEREO TRACK

NITA

BY JOHN COLTRANE

𝄢: C VERSION

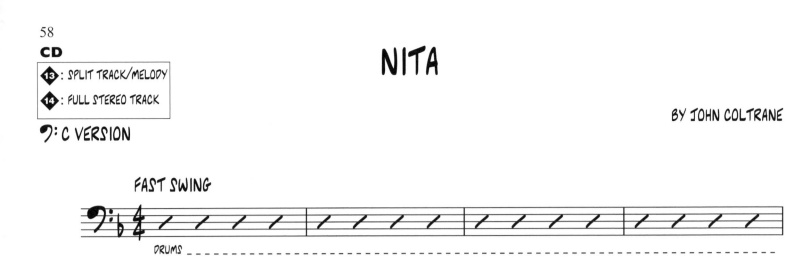

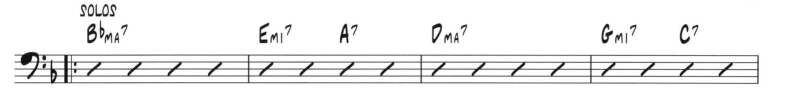

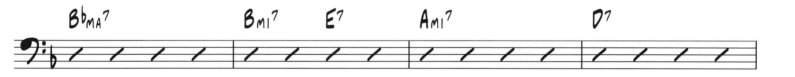

SATELLITE

BY JOHN COLTRANE

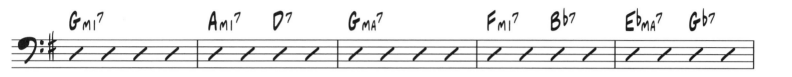

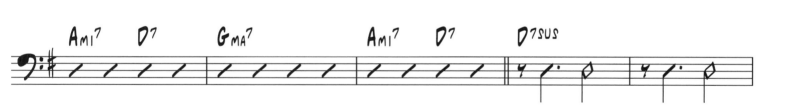

CD

26-2

BY JOHN COLTRANE

𝄢: C VERSION

MEDIUM SWING